This Book Belongs To:

Today's Date:

If you had to eat one food for every meal for an entire week, what would you choose?

What did you do today?

I went to get Jacky.

I went to the library.

We cam home.

What are some things you like to do for fun? Do you like to do these by yourself or with friends?

What is your favorite day of the week? Why?

Do you have a favorite bedtime story? If so, which one and why do you like it so much?

What is your favorite food? What is your least favorite food?

Do you like to cook? If so, who do you cook with and what do you like to make?

Would you rather be tall or short? Why?

If you could learn any foreign language, which one would you choose?

Describe your favorite animal at the zoo.

There is a blizzard outside and you have to stay indoors. Describe your day.

What would you like to do this summer? Have you ever done this before?

Are there any sports or hobbies you would like to try in the next year? If so, which ones?

What is your favorite holiday? Why is it your favorite?

If you just won the lottery, how would you spend the money?

If your favorite animal could talk, what would they say?

What is your favorite subject in school? Why? What is your least favorite? Why?

Imagine there is a large rainstorm right now. Is there anything special you would do?

Describe three things you should always do after school.

Who is your favorite teacher? Why are they so special?

If you were the President, what would you do to make people happier?

Pretend cats and dogs can fly. How would the world be different?

If you could have a super power, what would it be? What would you do with it?

Imagine you have a time machine. List 3 times and places you'd like to visit.

Do you prefer movies or tv shows? Why?

Explain why it's important to eat healthy and exercise.

Who is your hero? Why do you admire this person?

Pretend you are invisible for a day. What would you do?

What did you do last weekend?

Imagine you have a pet skunk. What would it be like? What would you name it?

Pretend you're going on a camping trip this weekend. What would you pack?

If you had a pet robot, what would they do? What would you name your robot?

What is your favorite thing to write?

Do you prefer walking or running? Explain.

What is your favorite kind of candy? How often do you eat it?

What are your favorite things to do at summer camp?

If you had a spaceship and could travel to any planet, where would you go?

If you could meet any past President, who would it be and why?

Do you prefer watching TV or reading a book? Why?

What does your Mom and Dad do for a living?

What is your favorite restaurant? What do you like to eat there?

Are you going to miss school during summer? Why or why not?

Pretend you could snap your fingers and go to any foreign country. Which one would you choose?

What is your favorite season? What do you like to do during this time?

What is your favorite ice cream flavor? Do you add toppings? Cone or cup?

When you don't have to go to school, what is your favorite thing to do?

Made in the USA
Middletown, DE
12 July 2020